Compassionate Prosperity

WHEN SUCCESS IS NOT ENOUGH

Andrea Putting

I0086209

Putting Words
publishing

Melbourne - Australia

Money makes the world go around.....or does it?

Business leaders and entrepreneurs are often driven by money however it's those that are driven by something greater than themselves, doing or giving something that can assist others, that's when success takes on a different meaning.

Andrea lives and breathes a selfless devotion to helping others in all walks of life from around the world. Her insight into human behaviour and her giving of time to those who seek her compassion and guidance has helped many people on their journey of discovery and prosperity.

Knowledge gained serves only one, knowledge shared serves thousands. Andrea continues her search for knowledge through her podcast whilst sharing with many others who tune in.

Compassionate prosperity can be achieved by everyone, especially with the guidance from this book and listening to Andrea's podcast.

Warren Tate – *Professional Speaker, Best-selling Author, Executive Communication and Presentation Coach.*

Philanthro-Capitalism: taking the best of philanthropy (love), jettisoning the worst (charity), combining it with the best of capitalism (free enterprise) and getting rid of the worst (greed). This is exactly what you'll find in Andrea Putting's new book Compassionate Prosperity. This book will allow you to dovetail your professional highest calling with your spiritual highest calling.

Frank McKinney - *7x Best-selling Author, including Aspire! How to Create Your Own Reality and Alter Your DNA.*

Contents

Dedicated to Mason and Zoey
and all the Future Revolutionist.

Preface

Compassionate Prosperity is of way to think about business that fits in the changing world. Yet, looking back in time, it reflects how society began. Our basic survival depended on us caring for each other and working together as a community. Was this forgotten in the quest for development and growth in the industrial world?

Just as that began with the Industrial Revolution, our return to what gives us a sense of purpose and fulfilment is a new revolution, the Social Mission Revolution.

Compassionate Prosperity represents what I have seen and heard through my podcast Social Mission Revolution. Magic seems to happen when people and businesses focus on being compassionate by embracing a social mission. They gain prosperity that is beyond profit. It is prosperity where all involved find satisfaction in their work-life and business. People work together with a renewed sense of excitement as they realise that what they do every day makes a difference.

When I developed my social mission, Chocolate and Coffee Day for Religious Harmony, something happened within me. By finding a purpose that had no apparent benefits to me personally, I discovered a drive within me that became a force of its own. Here was something I can't not do. It picked me up when I was down and got me out of bed. It gave me a reason to do things out of my comfort zone.

The fascination of "**I can't not do this**" led me on this journey. I started to recognise the difference between a business with a social mission and one that doesn't. As a result, Social Mission Revolution was born.

This book is an invitation to consider the legacy you want to live today and leave for generations to come. What is right for you at this time in your business? Where is it calling you to take it? What will it take for your business to be the influencer in your industry and the world? How can it be an authentic influence that will ripple throughout time and beyond?

Acknowledgements

I acknowledge and pay respect to the Wurundjeri Woi-wurrung people of the Kulin Nation, who are the Traditional Owners of the land where I live, work and find my inspiration. I pay my respects to Elders past, present and emerging of the Aboriginal and Torrens Strait Islanders. I acknowledge their deep connection to this land, water and the spirit of this place. I celebrate the stories, culture, and traditions of those who have led the way and taught us the importance of community and collaboration to build a better world.

Acknowledgement of country and the traditional owners has become a respectful practice in Australia. It is shared at official engagements and anywhere people meet. It reminds me of the influence that the elders of the past have had on my life. The Indigenous of Australia have the oldest culture in the world. They created their prosperity through working together. It may be a different type of prosperity that we may not recognise in our lives, yet concepts that we can draw from in the way we do business and community today. We can learn much from how they care for each other and the land on which we live.

I pay respects to the elders of the past in my traditions and communities. Their determinations, passions and commitment to their beliefs have inspired and shaped my life.

I pay respect to the elders of the present. Those who have inspired, guided and mentored me. For family and friends who walk this journey with me, who encourage and support me through all the crazy times that life has been throwing at us.

I pay respect to the emerging elders, who will lead our world in new ways that we can't foresee. The leaders of the future revolutions will change life as we know it for the betterment of all.

I pay respect to you, the reader. May you begin a ripple effect that will be acknowledged throughout time.

I especially pay respect and gratitude to my book writing mentor, Anna Von Zinner. Her guidance and expertise have made me a better writer and encouraged me to keep writing.

The true measure of your success
is in the lives you touch.

A business with a social mission inspires change, people, and its employees and their families.

CHAPTER 1

The Social Mission Revolution

Filling the view out of my office window, a golden elm tree stretches out its branches covered with fluorescent green leaves. I spend many hours sitting in reflection, gazing at it. Over the past 27 years, I have watched this tree grow from a small tree to today's giant. I have witnessed the changing of the seasons through the leaves and changing colours of this tree.

The leaves turn from vibrant green to a golden yellow, falling from the tree in Autumn, leaving its branches bare in Winter. Then in Spring, new life appears, buds and blossoms develop, and the leaves begin to sprout again. We have nurtured the tree as it became infested with the beetles of Dutch Elm Disease and have celebrated its return to its full glory.

Every Spring, our garden seems to be overrun by more and more sprouting elms. While we continue to remove these, I can't help pondering that a forest of elm trees would now surround us if left to its own devices.

The tree has a life of its own. It takes directions that we have no control over. We could try to control it if we felt inclined, trimming and shaping it. However, the beauty of the tree and its life force isn't one to bind and force into our imagined shape.

It seeks nothing but the light and water that sustain it. It gives of itself freely, expecting nothing in return. It nourishes a community of insects and birds. It provides shelter and shade from the weather. It offers a haven for my pet cockatoo to play under and an imaginary world for my grandchildren to play in. It is a source of continual inspiration for my writing and my work.

Social mission is like this tree. It gives of itself and asks for nothing in return; it is nurtured and nourished by its journey. In the same way, the more a social mission gives, the more it grows. The more it grows, the more it has to give.

As it gives, a social mission develops its own ecosystem. A social mission cannot live in isolation. It needs this giving and receiving to survive. It needs to grow and sprout new life to spread its message. It needs to offer itself up to others to expand its purpose. When a business surrenders to the light that calls it, to the life that it supports, a social mission emerges, and it becomes all that it can be.

It has no agenda other than to be and follow the light that guides it. When it does, it becomes an **authentic influence** to all those around it and the world.

WHAT IS THE SOCIAL MISSION REVOLUTION?

A Social Mission is a not-for-profit cause undertaken to help society. An organisation undertakes a Social Mission to make a difference in the world. It is something that a business organisation primarily has a higher calling to do. The benefits are beyond that of the organisation or business; it brings a deep sense of purpose and passion to all stakeholders. (The stakeholders are all interested parties in the business, such as the investors, the business owners, the employees, customers and suppliers.)

A social mission can take on many faces, as represented by the plethora of examples on the *Social Mission Revolution* podcast I produce. It can vary from:

- contributing time to charitable events;
- giving a percentage of profits;
- getting a team together to volunteer;
- starting your own cause or movement;
- founding a social enterprise that supports community development.

There are as many ways to have, express and explore social missions as there are people.

Social missions are embraced by individuals, groups, communities, organisations, businesses and corporations. It spans all sectors, walks of life, cultures, and countries.

A business with a social mission inspires change, people, employees, and their families. It creates a following of people who believe in the cause. They become devoted followers of the brand because it is serving humanity. It is an **authentic influence**.

In business and corporations, it is often referred to as Corporate Social Responsibility (CSR). In some circumstances, governments mandate that they must have a CSR, but others see it as an opportunity to give back to the communities that support them.

To be involved in the Social Mission Revolution, all that is required is a desire to make a difference and do something greater than yourself.

The word "revolution" means "a radical and pervasive change in society and social structure." Those businesses who embrace the Social Mission Revolution have an overriding sense of wanting to do something more than they have been doing.

Our society has transformed into a materialistic world, where everything is "me" based and "what can I achieve to get more for me." Our focus has now changed, and it has influenced how we do business. Now society is becoming more outwardly focused, looking at what companies or organisations can do for others, in addition to providing their products or services.

Revolution also refers to "a turning around as if returning back to a starting point." By focusing on a social mission, we are returning to who we truly are. In South Africa, they use the word – *Ubuntu*, which means "I am because you are." It focuses on working together to create the community that is one and a world that we all want. For humanity to survive, we must care for each other.

Like my elm tree, the Social Mission Revolution creates an ecosystem of giving freely, and in return, it offers us growth and development of who we truly are. It surrenders to its purpose and follows the light that calls it. When we nourish and nurture the other, we can become a greater version of ourselves, as does the tree. Our seeds spread like the elm, our message is heard, our businesses flourish, and our community is nourished. A forest is grown.

You become an **authentic influence**.

When you take action on what speaks
so strongly to your heart that you
cannot not do it, you will have
authentic influence and will
leave a legacy worth living.

CHAPTER 2

Embracing Authentic Influence

The alarm has gone off, and it's time to get out of bed. The new day is before you. How does it feel? Are you excited about what lies ahead, or is it another dreary day of the same old thing?

For many people getting up in the morning isn't easy. They just want to throw the alarm clock across the room, pull the blankets back over their heads and hide from the world. We all have times like that.

What does it take to turn that feeling around?

How can you look forward to the new day, horizon, and next opportunity?

We are conditioned to think that success lies in how much money and power we have or the bricks and mortar legacy we may leave. It keeps us on the treadmill of forever striving, struggling for more, and searching for that elusive pot of gold at the end of the rainbow or the Holy Grail. We always want something else, more, more, more.

The sad truth is that you may never find something that fulfils your life or that feeling that your business had entirely captured that big vision you had when you started it. Where is that something that gives you the sense that "My business is important because it makes a difference in people's lives, and that's what matters." Your business just doesn't quite feel satisfying. It doesn't feel like it is the **authentic influence** you want it to be in the world.

What if we've got it wrong? We've turned our lives upside down, looking outside ourselves to find the answer.

We are told the answer lies in the "Why." Search for the reason you do what you do. Why did you start your business? Simon Sinek, author and inspirational speaker, tells us to "Start with Why." But what if the truth is deeper than that. What if the answer lies **beyond the why**?

What if your business dream's true purpose and fulfilment only comes when you let go of all your agenda? What if you allowed yourself and your employees to go deeper and deeper, to be guided by something greater than yourself? What if you discovered something beyond what you could have dreamed of that would take your business to the next level that is more meaningful and powerful?

What if you let something wholly new and unexpected flow into your business that you just *cannot not* do? This is the power of journeying **beyond the why**.

Ian Ugarte is a successful property developer. The business was going great. Financially he was set. However, something was missing. Even though he had all the spoils of being successful, he realised he was not happy after achieving his goals. Gradually he dove into a depression and was at the point of thinking of ending his life. Fortunately, his family and friends couldn't help but notice the change in him and sat with him to work through this. The work he was doing no longer had meaning for him. How could he change what he was good at and bring new meaning and purpose?

He took a fresh look at the property market and saw the flaws. With the soaring prices of housing, many people were struggling just to afford the rent. Often people find themselves in difficult situations and face possible homelessness unless they can find more affordable quality living arrangements. Yet this was not being addressed in the market. Homes in Australia are typically 3- or 4-bedroom homes, with a considerable percentage of them now being single or couple occupancy. It didn't make sense. There are times in people's lives when they need something smaller.

Ian turned his focus and became an advocate for affordable housing. He now builds and develops smaller, affordable co-living homes that people enjoy living in. Now all of his business decisions have to pass two standards. They have to benefit the community and make good financial sense.

Ian's story is the epitome of what the Social Mission Revolution is all about. In redesigning business, it offers benefits to the community while bringing a greater sense of satisfaction and fulfilment on a personal level to all who work there. www.socialmissionrevolution.com/Ian-Ugarte

Over the past five years, I have explored what it means to people and businesses to have a social mission. I have looked at the facts, the figures, and, most importantly, its effect on the individual, business, and community.

The stories I have gathered through my podcast, *Social Mission Revolution,* have truly been inspiring. Some businesses have taken the risk to hear the calling and just step up and take the chance for no other reason than to make a difference.

I have had the privilege of interviewing the most passionate people with remarkable businesses. Their drive to get up every morning to make a difference, go against the odds, and do something with no monetary reward is inspiring. In this, we find true **authentic influence.**

WHAT IS AUTHENTIC INFLUENCE?

The world is filled with noise. We are constantly bombarded with messages, with people trying to get our attention. They want to influence us. They want us to buy their goods. Do things their way. Think this way. Copy me. I have the answers you seek. Is this what you want to be? Is this the type of influence you want in the world? Or do you want **authentic influence?**

Being an influencer in the 21st century has become defined by how many social media followers a person has. Actors, musicians, sportspeople and absolute nobodies suddenly become megastars with a clever strategy to gain more followers. However, how are they influencing others? Is it real influence that makes a difference, or is it just about being famous and selling the latest thing? Is this the kind of influence you want?

Growing up, my siblings and I learned many essential things in life while sitting in the back pews at church. We learned how to play battleships and hangman, make paper aeroplanes, origami paper games, and sign language. Like most children and young people, sitting still in church for an hour was not on my agenda. We had to keep occupied somehow.

However, somewhere along the lines, something did stay with me. All the ministers are volunteers at our church, so they take turns presiding over services. A few years ago, I realised the influence that one of these ministers had on my life.

Ted had a consistent message. We all knew it well. We knew that his message was going to be on earth stewardship. He was a true greenie long before the term was ever coined. He would teach and preach about the importance of caring for the environment. There were always flipcharts (technology of the 60s) which made it a little more interesting for the younger audience.

I remember stories of whales, trees, spaceships, and living on the growing edge. Ted influenced my young mind and those of others around me. We grew up knowing that we had to take care of the earth. We had to think about unheard of things, like recycling, waste control and alternative energy. These were important. This is God's world, and it is our responsibility to take care of it.

When I started to contemplate this, I began to see something that I can only frame as being an **authentic influence**. I could see this ripple effect. I saw how it influenced the way I raised my family, the care we took in life not to be wasteful and to recycle.

I then started to see in my children that this was something powerful that had influenced them. They are always mindful of these things, and they influence others around them, in their workplace, amongst their friends and communities and in their homes. My grandchildren are growing up with the same ethos.

Ted's influence will continue; it will grow and expand to others. He lived his message through and through. He was an example of his values; he never stopped. He lived his life humbly dedicated to his mission.

This is the kind of influence I want to have in the world. As a leader, speaker, author, minister, and grandmother, I want to have an **authentic influence** that makes a difference to others and ultimately impacts the world.

I see many leaders trying hard to have influence. They want to influence their workplace, their communities and the world. They want their business to be the influence that gains attention. However, unless it is an **authentic influence**, it just doesn't stick.

When you embrace taking on a social mission, you need to do it for the right reasons. It can't come from a place of manipulation so it will lift your bottom line of productivity, innovation and profit. The world will see through that. It needs to come from the heart. It needs to be the soul of the business. Only from this place will you become an **authentic influence**.

While we have numerous reasons to embrace a social mission, we don't need to look very far to see that the world is crying out for significant change and great leaders. A myriad of causes and needs within the world are waiting to be addressed.

There is something that every business can do to make this world a better place. There is something that every organisation can do to create the world that we want to live in. Social Mission builds within a business or organisation a legacy worth living and leaving.

This is not something to be put off for a "better time". This is for now! Whatever circumstances, no matter how busy, how important all those things you have scheduled are, there is something that you can do, and you must do, NOW! When you incorporate a social mission into a business, it gives everyone in that business a reason to get up in the morning and keep going. It will inspire every decision and every motive. It will keep you going when life gets tough. That magic ingredient is needed in your business to bring fulfilment and unleash your business's ultimate impact on the world.

CREATING A LEGACY

Legacy is thought of as how much money or power you can leave behind for your loved ones. You work hard to build your business. In the end, it has equity that can be sold or continued for further generations.

In Japan, there is a business that has been family-owned since 705. All 52 generations of one family have run the family hotel of Nishiyama Onsen Keiunkan. That's quite a legacy! Is this the kind of legacy you wish to leave, or is it something else?

While it is nice to leave financial security for our loved ones, does it give them the sense of pride that they will share stories for generations to come? Or is this a narrow way of thinking about what a legacy is?

The word legacy originated in the late 14th century from Medieval Latin and meant "body of persons sent on a mission." Legacy in these terms gives us something different to think about. When our work feels like we have set out on a mission, the legacy could extend far beyond just leaving financial security for your family.

The stories shared on the *Social Mission Revolution Podcast* that you will read in this book speak of these far-reaching legacies and **authentic influence**. These businesses are living a legacy that changes lives and changes the world.

They have taken on compassionate projects that impact the lives of others. Their purpose is not to make money from these projects but to serve their communities. They do it alongside their daily business. For some, it is a once-a-year project; for others, it is a part of their everyday mission, and they employ someone specifically to make sure that they grow this legacy.

Social missions through business come in all shapes and sizes, from raising money and collecting donations to volunteering time or services (pro-bono work). For others, it is the impetus to start the business in the first place as a social enterprise. They all have in common that they touch a more significant number of lives, and the impact is profound. They change lives and whole communities, filling empty spaces and empowering people along the way. This legacy of authentic influence creates the ultimate impact of your business.

Wherever we see a gap in the world, wherever we see an injustice, wherever we think something should be different, it is up to us to be at the forefront of these places. As businesses and organisations, we have the infrastructures, the contacts, and the opportunities to make this difference in the world.

As a business owner, Chief Executive Officer or Managing Director, you have the power to make a difference while improving your business. When you take action on what speaks so strongly to your heart that you *cannot not* do it, you will have **authentic influence** and leave a legacy worth living.

A business with a social mission
will draw to it, naturally,
a following of consumers
who believe in the mission.

CHAPTER 3

Social Mission in Business

Currently, we have an additional pandemic to COVID. We have a pandemic of disengagement in the workplace. People are going to work, day in, day out and just not feeling it. This is costing businesses dearly.

According to the Gallup *State of the Global Workplace Report 2021 Engagement Report*, 80% of employees worldwide are disengaged or disinterested in the workplace. What does this mean for businesses? It means that employees are going to work and just doing the minimum.

Employees have lost interest in pursuing anything further in the business. They don't offer ideas or suggestions. They don't care about the customer service or whether the business is highly successful, just as long as it keeps going, so they get their pay packet at the end of the week.

The growth of the business is not their concern. Employees are only going to do precisely what they are paid for and nothing more.

Research conducted in 2015 by Michael Henderson, a corporate anthropologist, showed that seven out of ten businesses don't reach their highest potential. The similarities in the Gallup and Henderson findings hardly seem like a coincidence.

A business has no chance of reaching its highest potential – having its ultimate impact or being an **authentic influence** – if its employees aren't engaged in what they are doing and aren't engaged in growing the business. They won't look for, recognise, or act upon opportunities that might be there.

The business loses out in all vital areas for survival in the business world — productivity, innovation and profit. The chances of the business being an **authentic influence** are non-existent.

What if we can combine the deep longing to make a difference that fills our heart and soul, that inspires us to get up in the morning and work at a far more motivated level with going to work each day?

How would that affect the day-to-day running of a business? How would that impact employee engagement?

And how would it affect those vital bottom lines of productivity, innovation, and profit?

Imagine this. There is two coffee shops side by side. Which one do you choose to buy your coffee from? They both have equally as good coffee at the same price. However, the coffee shop on the right has a social mission. For every cup of coffee sold, a child in a developing country receives clean drinking water for the day. Which coffee shop are you going to choose for your daily cuppa? The one on the right or the one on the left?

Overwhelmingly, people choose the coffee shop on the right.

Let's look at the consequences of this. A social impact is made with every cup of coffee. Children receive the essential water they need to survive. The staff are more engaged as they feel good about every cup of coffee they sell. When they go to work, they make a difference beyond just the people they serve every day. Customers feel good about their spending and come back time and time again. It makes good business sense, as they sell more coffee than the shop next door.

This is a story that **Steve Pipe** shared when he came on the *Social Mission Revolution* podcast. He talked about how easy it is for businesses to make an impact through B1G1. www.socialmissionrevolution.com/Steve-Pipe

The truth is, it costs very little for the coffee shop to make this impact. When you look at this example, why wouldn't you, as a business owner, not get involved in social mission? Making your business sustainable and keeping employees and clientele engaged is a must in the 21st century. It helps to create prosperity and legacy.

The reasons for social mission go beyond just financial prosperity. It helps to bring purpose and satisfaction to your life.

When a business engages in a social mission, its employees develop emotional engagement. Being emotionally engaged gives going to work each day a new meaning for employees. It is now not just about themselves; what they do matters. It really matters. It creates opportunities for others. It feeds people. It saves the environment, or whatever the business's mission is.

It speaks to all and gives them that deeper reason for going to work. It is no longer so much about sales figures but creating an impact. What effect has a business's employees had by going to work today?

WHY DOES SOCIAL MISSION IN BUSINESS WORK?

The inbuilt desire to make a difference is underlying in all our lives. Creating the opportunity for employees to fulfil this desire contributes to their sense of well-being, with the outcome of greater engagement in the workplace.

Dr Stephen Post, founder of the Institute of Research into Unlimited Love and co-author of *Why Good Things Happen to Good People*, has studied the benefits and links between altruism, compassion, happiness, healing, and health. In *It's good to be good: 2011 5th annual scientific report on health, happiness and helping others,* he points out that happiness, health and even longevity are benefits that have been reported in more than 50 investigations using a variety of methodologies.

Dr Post also refers to the 2010 survey conducted by United Health Care and Volunteer Match in the US in his book. In this survey of 4,582 American adults, 41 per cent volunteered an average of two hours per week; 68 per cent of volunteers agree that volunteering "has made me feel physically healthier", and 96 per cent say volunteering "makes people happier." In addition, the survey results indicated that volunteers have less trouble sleeping, less anxiety, and better friendships and social networks.

Based on the scientific research, Dr Post concludes that giving and even just thinking about giving in a spirit of generosity are linked to health and well-being, and altruism is associated with a substantial reduction in mortality rates and is, therefore, linked to longevity.

Mixing business with social mission creates happier and healthier employees and businesses. When people find fulfilment at work, it ripples into all aspects of life, and we have a better world. Your business becomes an **authentic influence**.

When teams start to function with purpose and desire to make a difference, magic happens. Here is where new visions for what can be start to emerge. Where the future starts to unfold, add to this the beauty of each person feeling a sense of ownership to new projects, and more significant commitment begins to flourish.

The fact is that the employees are your business. They are the ones who will be your greatest champions if they find what we all desperately seek, a sense of purpose.

It is essential to recognise that a workplace is not just where the work gets done. A workplace is where people live, dream, and find a sense of purpose – or not.

If they can't find deep purpose in their work, they are not challenged or motivated. They will be looking for something else that will somehow fulfil that deep longing in their soul to make a difference in their world. The workplace is where people spend the majority of their time and energy. If they are not happy in this place, everyone suffers in every area of their lives.

Many businesses take on Corporate Social Responsibility to varying degrees. For many, it is just ticking the box. They decide (or it is regulated for them) to give a specific profit percentage to a charitable fund or organisation. They send the money, and that is that. It might look good on paper; however, the employees don't know what it is about and are not inspired by it. Meanwhile, the business struggles to keep employees interested, and they struggle with that all-important PIP – Productivity, Innovation and Profit. They are hardly the **authentic influence** that they could be.

The changing face of consumerism can help give us a direction in which to steer our business's social mission. Consumers are voting with their wallets. The rise of B-Corporations is a prime example.

Certified B Corporation businesses meet the highest standard of ethical, social and environmental performance. The B Corp community works toward reduced inequality, lower levels of poverty, a healthier environment, stronger communities, and the creation of more high-quality jobs with dignity and purpose.

By harnessing the power of business, B Corps use profits and growth as a means to a greater end: a positive impact on their employees, communities, and the environment. Consumers look to this certification to find companies to support who align with their values and ideas. I spoke with **Karen Porter**, the founder of The Benefit Consultants, about what it means to be a B Corp business; here is the link www.SocialMissionRevolution.com/Karen-Porter.

People demand much more of the products they buy and the companies that produce them. A study conducted by research firm McCrindle, on behalf of Fairtrade Australia and New Zealand, found eight in ten shoppers would be more likely to purchase a product that supports someone in need rather than one that did not have a charitable aspect.

We can see evidence of this in companies such as Etiko, a company that sells ethically sourced and made apparel, footwear and sports balls. "We wanted to be 100% confident the apparel and footwear we were buying for our family hadn't been made by a child or some poor worker being ripped off in a developing country. At the time, this didn't exist, so we created it. We constantly set the bar for upholding and campaigning the human rights of people working in traditionally exploitative industry supply chains." Consumers worldwide seek out Etiko as they want to ensure that the products they purchase align with their values.

The consumer view is that "If I'm going to buy a product and the choice is to buy one with a social conscience, then, of course, that is the one I'm going to buy."

In developing a culture of social mission, a business finds that spark and fulfils the longing for something greater within all stakeholders – business, management, employees, consumers, society and the environment alike. It has the opportunity to influence the world in a positive and meaningful way – as an **authentic influence**.

A business takes on a life of its own and develops its own calling. To discover this greater purpose, we need to let go of all our own agendas, all that seems logical and our personal sense of why. We then need to allow it to take us **beyond the why**, where we can awaken the soul of a business.

Here we can discover something far greater than we could ever imagine that will ignite passion amongst employees and consumers. Here new visions, inspirations and innovations will unfold, and an enduring legacy with **authentic influence** will be created.

This is where the Social Mission Revolution comes alive. While there is plenty of evidence that businesses with a social conscience and mission are more productive and profitable, it is not likely to be successful if taken up with this agenda. Having a social mission needs to be at the very heart and soul of the business. It comes from this deep longing within each one of us to do something meaningful in our lives: to make a difference and leave a legacy.

Genuinely successful incorporation of a social mission occurs when it involves the whole business. This means not just the owner or CEO coming in and saying, "This is what we will do," but instead working together with management and staff, possibly including customers and other stakeholders. Using this approach, everyone feels ownership of the project and will be enthusiastic about implementing the changes that follow.

Finding what social mission a business is being called to stand up for will evolve from listening to the emerging future of the business. When people come together with intention and start to share their stories and concerns, images emerge of the direction to follow. Of course, there are many possibilities.

This process requires deep listening where it is possible to go **beyond the why** — to each other, to the community and to what social mission wants to emerge. Once ideas start to formulate, excitement builds about what is possible. Exploring these and creating prototypes that can be started straight away helps keep the momentum going. It is about diving into something, trying it out without it having to be perfect. Then as we go, we review, reflect and improve until the perfect social mission for your business is found and implemented.

Some of the benefits of such a process are the building of relationships, a greater sense of purpose in the day-to-day activities in the business, increased loyalty amongst employees and customers, and the building of a true legacy.

Taking on a social mission has many advantages, for you personally and for the business.

As a business with a social mission, you stand out in the world. You are a leader who thinks of other people, and your actions are inspirational to them. You inspire others to look outside of themselves and how they can do something worthwhile beyond their job. You are an **authentic influence**. This is a business where people want to work.

Having a social mission shows that you, as a business or organisation, are committed to the community and have more substance than just making money. It shows that you have a heart.

A business with a social mission will draw to it, naturally, a following of consumers who believe in the mission. It will create a positive and charismatic attraction to your business. The influence you have won't be superficial; it will be deep and meaningful that, in itself, becomes a legacy – an **authentic influence.**

> *"What we have done for ourselves dies with us; what we have done for others, and the world remains and is immortal." – Albert Pike.*

Joining the Social Mission Revolution will inspire and motivate you, those who work with you and society. Together we can make the difference that the world is begging for and leave an enduring legacy that our children and we can be proud of.

It is time to discover how you can have **authentic influence** and unleash your ultimate impact on the world.

CHAPTER 4

Discovering the Social Mission Revolution

When you watch the *Social Mission Revolution Podcast* on YouTube, you will see a beautiful heart quilt behind me that my mother made many years ago. She lovingly selected the fabrics, cut them out and pieced them together to create a masterpiece that, to her, represented her daughter. I loved it and appreciated it but didn't understand the heart at the time. Over the years, sitting in my office, I started to see that this quilt represents who I am.

A quilt is an excellent metaphor for our lives and the stories we stitch together, piece by piece. We choose the colour and the tones. Sometimes the individual pieces aren't very appealing; however, when we bring them together, they create the masterpiece of our life.

It was a joy and a blessing to be a stay-at-home mother for our two children. My husband and I made the decision together knowing that life wouldn't always be easy. There would be financial and emotional struggles; however, it was a sacrifice we were willing to make.

When the children went to school, so did I. It was time for me to expand my horizons, and never being one to do anything by halves, I took on two Advanced Diplomas at the same time: one in Naturopathy and the other in Homoeopathy. It was a tough four and a half years of juggling children and homelife with full-time study. My husband was also expanding his horizons. A significant project came his way that would cement him as the expert in his field. This meant longer hours and even more weekend work for him. He worked 80 hours a week for over a year. The stresses on him were enormous. He had no time for himself, no time for the children, no time for me.

This time highlighted the pressures that work-life places on people and families. There is no time for those essential things that we should all take for granted: family life, relationships, spiritual life, exercise, friends, community. Often, people get stuck in that everyday grind and don't enjoy their work. They find no real sense of fulfilment or purpose in what they are doing, and they bring home feelings of despair to their family. They no longer have the time or energy to pick themselves up and do those things that give their lives meaning. They can't even contemplate the idea of sharing in community life and giving of themselves by serving. They have nothing left. That will all have to wait until retirement.

Now that my education was completed, it was time for me to venture into the business world. My son suggested that I could start an online health business. The internet was all shiny and new. I felt like a pioneer in this world. It was last century, in what I call the dinosaur era of the internet. Only dial-up services were available, no Google, no PayPal, no Facebook and certainly no WordPress. I had to create everything from scratch. I learnt new languages – HTML, CGI and ASP. It took time for people to accept this new technology. Entering their credit card details on a website was still very scary.

 Finding my niche in a very hard to get substance – Apricot Kernels – cemented my business in the new marketplace. With the help of my children (who at this time were teenagers), we packed hundreds of kilograms of apricot kernels every week to send out to customers who used them in their cancer prevention regimes. The business was beginning to flourish. I was becoming well-known for my articles (pre-blogs) and the information I was providing.

Then came the moment when I sat and looked at my dining room table and thought, "Is this why I studied for all those years?" I had lost my passion. It was lying buried beneath the boxes of apricot kernels and the tediousness of the day-to-day work. While I was making a difference in people's lives, I still felt like there was something more significant for me to be doing in the world.

Divine providence stepped in. My supplier stopped supplying. Now, I had to make a hard decision. I sold the business to someone who was able to keep the supply going. My children were grown, and it was time for me to step out of my home office and comfort zone.

What next? Why not get a job? Everyone else does it. It can't be that bad. I longed to work with other people, to find that sense of community that my soul needed. I wanted to connect with the power of people working together towards one vision.

I found a job that I was good at, and I made an impact. However, I had to learn that my place was not to be the one with the big visions. That was for someone else. Somewhere along the line, I stopped being whole. I now focused all of my energy on my job. There was nothing left for all the things that were important to me. I wholly immersed myself in someone else's vision and dream. It overtook my life.

As time went by, the cracks started to appear. I looked around and saw the truth. People were working hard yet feeling empty. They had no real purpose driving their actions.

While this takes a personal toll on the business owner and employees, it also takes a toll on the business. How can a business be an **authentic influence** in its industry and the world when there is no unity pulling together the pieces behind the scenes?

This is when employees lose interest in their work; performance suffers, and profit falls. Owners and employees alike begin to burn out. Bullying occurs. The business's values, vision, and mission are lost in a pile of worthlessness. The business may continue; however, it will never reach its highest potential or have its ultimate impact on the world. It certainly won't be an **authentic influence**.

By now, I was on edge. I was falling apart. I was drowning in the negativity that I found myself in at work. Then that moment happened that pulled me out of my downward slide.

It was 5:15 pm on a Friday, and my work week was done. I was lost in despair. I stood at the train crossing; the boom gate was down, the lights were flashing, and the warning signal was chiming. The express train was speeding towards me. "It would be so easy to step in front of that train." Whoa, where did that thought come from? This is not who I am. I had lost myself.

It was time for something to change. I had to move on.

As I stepped away, I could see everything from a new perspective. I have seen and experienced the world of business from three different aspects. The family is waiting on the sidelines for the crumbs of time and energy given by the partner working long hours. The business owner who lost her passion in the day-to-day grind. The employee who lost their purpose and found no fulfilment in the workplace and, as a result, became disengaged.

There had to be a better way. This was my mission. My search was on. The answers we seek often come in unexpected ways. When we have put the work in and are ready to step into something new, it appears.

It was the 15th of December 2014, and I sat glued to my computer screen watching the news. It appeared that the unthinkable was happening right here in Australia. A gunman carrying a Jihadist flag took patrons and staff hostage at the Lindt Chocolate Café in Sydney. Sadly, two innocent victims and the gunman died.

In the aftermath, we collectively held our breath. Would there be retaliation against the Muslim community, who had nothing to do with this? Slowly, quietly, a roar erupted on social media with #Iwillridewithyou. All over Sydney and Australia, people were offering to ride the train, the bus or the ferry with Muslims to ensure that they felt safe and protected.

Instead of people lashing out at Muslims, we had an outpouring of love and acceptance. This is the Australia that I am proud of and want to live in.

This event sat with me for ten months. I pondered it. I looked for changes in community attitudes. I wanted to see more. I wanted to see that people were connecting and treating each other with more love and acceptance. Then I questioned, "Why should we wait until there is another tragedy before we speak up? Why can't we do something that makes a statement that we want to live in peace and harmony where all are treated equally, all of the time?"

Then came the moment when I asked, "When is Chocolate and Coffee Day?" At that moment, I discovered my social mission, and the seed of the Social Mission Revolution was planted.

Chocolate and Coffee Day for Religious Harmony is a simple concept that is easy to participate in and enjoy. The basic idea is to reach out to someone different from you and share life's simple pleasures, chocolate, coffee, and conversation. Here, we get to know the other person and learn about their stories, lives, struggles, and joys. Here is where we start to walk in their shoes, feel empathy and break down the barriers that divide people and community.

Over the past seven years, Chocolate and Coffee Day for Religious Harmony has been shared worldwide in homes, coffee shops, retirement villages, churches, schools, online, workplaces, organisations and anywhere people gather. People have met together in small and large groups to make the statement that they want to live in a world where all are treated equally.

The inevitable question came, "Why is it just Chocolate and Coffee Day? Why can't we have Chocolate and Coffee every day?" And so, Chocolate and Coffee Breaks was conceived. The journey continues as I encourage people to take the stand for equality for all. Here was the way that I could have an **authentic influence.**

Chocolate, Coffee and Conversation have spilled over into every area of my life. I find a way to incorporate it into all my work. When you invite me in to do a talk, seminar or workshop, somewhere in the mix will be the joy of sharing chocolate, coffee and conversation. The power that these three simple pleasures of life have when they are combined is amazing.

This brings us to the question of "Why?" Start with why they say. If I started with why, would I have ever found this something that moves me and picks me up when nothing else can?

I had to let go of my agendas. Let go of my stories. Let go of my why. When I allowed myself to be guided by something **beyond the why** I was able to find this something that I **cannot not** do. Here I found something that drives me. It picks me up when I am down. It makes me defy all of my uncertainties and do whatever it takes.

Once you have this type of certainty, there is no turning back. You have heard your calling, and you have to give it your all; nothing else will do. Nothing else gives you a sense of satisfaction or fulfilment. You have to go **beyond the why**. Here you will have your ultimate impact on the world. You will be an **authentic influence**.

Why would it speak so strongly to me that all people are treated fairly and justly? Why do I get worked up at a drop of a hat when I see or hear of prejudice? I am a white Christian Australian woman raised in the White Australia Policy era. I have never been the victim of prejudice, but this is something that speaks so strongly to me that I *cannot not* take a stand against prejudice. I have to make this statement. I have to reach out to others. I have to make a change in the world.

You search for your why to inspire you. But the answers often lie deeper. We need to go **beyond the why**. We need to let go of our agendas and allow the future to emerge. We need to listen to our businesses and communities as their own identities and hear what they are saying and where they are calling us to go, so our businesses can have **authentic influence** and its ultimate impact. We need to connect to the heart space and the spirit that feeds us.

As I continued to piece together the quilt of my life, my eyes were opened to the power of Social Mission.

Social mission is a powerful tool for business. It brings people together. It inspires them to be more productive and innovative. It brings purpose and fulfilment into the workplace.

WHY SOCIAL MISSION?

Changing the world by yourself or as a single organisation isn't an easy path to take, and we don't have to.

There are so many ways that we can have our ultimate impact on the world and become an **authentic influence** that touches the lives of others. Many businesses partner with other organisations, or charities or give percentages of profits where it counts. When we work together, the impact is more substantial and more powerful. There is so much potential in businesses and organisations embracing the concept of a social mission.

For many people going to work each day is a chore that must be done. There aren't many people who are passionate about their work in a way that drives them, that keeps them excited and motivated. As mentioned earlier, the research by Gallup shows that 80% of all Australian (and global) employees are disengaged and/or dissatisfied in the workplace. This leaves precious few who care about and have an interest in the outcomes of a business.

HOW CAN SOCIAL MISSION HELP?

When people see that they are involved in something greater than themselves, they become inspired and motivated. They want to work; they want to be there. They know what they are doing makes a difference.

Knowing that their work will help someone else in some way can be a catalyst for more extraordinary things happening within a business. This is when a business becomes more than a business. It becomes a place where passionate changemakers are connected, unified to work together, where people are excited to be, united in a vision and a purpose. It is where they discover themselves and discover community or not.

When a business has a passionate mission, teams find absolute joy and passion in working with others. They share ideas and share dreams. They work more productively and become more profitable, as their work has the greatest pay-off of all time – fulfilment and satisfaction. The knowledge that they have made a difference and that what they do counts keeps them going through the ups and downs. They have the opportunity to become an **authentic influence**.

According to research by Glavas, A., and Kelley, K. (2014) the effects of perceived corporate social responsibility on employees), there is a direct relationship between a business having a social mission, employee engagement and satisfaction in their work.

Social mission in business is not just a "nice to have" in these times. It is a "must-have" if your business is to be a business of greatness, a business that stands out from the rest and lives and leaves a legacy – a satisfying business.

Consumers prefer companies that make a positive impact on the world. Eighty-three per cent of US consumers want more of the products and services they use to benefit causes (2010 Cone Cause Evolution Study conducted by Cone Communications), and 62% of global consumers will switch brands if one works with "good causes" and the other does not.

In some countries, there is a move to make it mandatory to be involved in Corporate Social Responsibility, often as a percentage of profitable income. While this is a great initiative that does a lot for the community, it can be seen as an obligation to be met. When something is done just out of obligation, it can be done in bitterness or resentment. It does nothing for the business or for the community that works there.

Social mission allows a business to do more, and become an **authentic influence** in the world while providing the business with the impetus to be more innovative, profitable, and productive. The next chapter shares stories of businesses, entrepreneurs and ordinary people who have embraced the Social Mission Revolution and seen the benefits firsthand.

The *Social Mission Revolution* podcast has given me great insight into what it means to people to work where the business has a social mission that they can embrace. I have seen how it helps to keep everyone motivated and inspired in their daily lives. It helps them connect deeper with their business or employment because the more they achieve in their daily work, the more they can give to something that matters to them at a deeper core level. It is what makes their life feel worthwhile.

This is what you and your business have been looking for. It is time to join the revolution – the Social Mission Revolution.

Sometimes a new idea will
blossom from unexpected
places and in unexpected ways.

CHAPTER 5

Social Mission in Action

So far, we've looked at why a social mission is vital for businesses and their employees. You want to be an **authentic influence**, and you feel the calling to build or incorporate a social mission into your business.

But what does a social mission look like?

There are many examples of businesses that are expressing their **authentic influence** on the *Social Mission Revolution Podcast*. Each one of them is a unique expression of the people involved and the business they represent. We all have different ways to serve, giving according to our passions, skills, and capacity in time, energy, and resources.

The stories that follow show examples of the wide variety of ways to serve. One might inspire the beginning of your business's social mission.

Donation

Many businesses find that the best way to participate in associal mission is to contribute financially to a cause or causes that align with their business values. There are a variety of ways and levels of involvement possible.

Daphne Kapetas is the founder of LAJOIE SKIN. With 40 years of experience in the cosmetic industry, she developed a natural product that provides relief from chaffing and found the product did more than that. With a giving heart, Daphne finds ways to serve in whatever she is doing, so she had to find a way to give within her business for it to have true meaning for her. The answer is simple. LAJOIE SKIN has regular sales events, where all the proceeds from the event will go to a designated charity. In doing this, Daphne finds joy and purpose in her business that helps keep her going. www.SocialMissionRevolution.com/Daphne-Kapetas

Annemarie Manders is very community-minded. Being a part of her local community and supporting local organisations gives her a sense of purpose. Annemarie's lavender farm, Warratina, in the Yarra Valley, near Melbourne, is more than a lovely place to visit and have afternoon tea. When the lavender drying season is over, the sheds become home to various craft exhibitions where all the entry fees are donated to groups such as the CFA (Country Fire Association). Through this, she has contributed to purchasing essential equipment for saving lives. The exhibitions bring together local craftspeople, giving them the opportunity to share their talents with the community.

www.SocialMissionRevolution.com/Annemarie-Manders

Emily and Iliano Ciardiello's business, Foil Me, provides the foils used by hairdressers for colouring hair. The hairdressing clients sit for an hour or so with aluminium foil pieces on their heads while looking in the mirror in the salon. Emily, a former English and Italian high school teacher, had an idea to use her talents as an artist. She started designing pictures to go on the foils. They brightened the experience for the clients and the hairdressers and are a talking point. A new idea was born to use these printed foils to raise awareness and as a fundraiser for charities. A donation is made to the designated charity for each box of these specially printed foils.

www.SocialMissionRevolution.com/E-and-I-Ciardiello

Cascie Kambouris wanted to start a charity. As she was pondering what she could do that would make a significant impact, someone said to her, "There is no amount of funding you can acquire that will change the world. You need money to make the change." So, her thoughts went to how she could support charities that already exist. Her business, The Hope Initiative, sells engraved bangles with messages of hope and inspiration. The business supports three different charities per financial quarter. Cascie wanted the customers to connect with the purposes of the charities and the gifts to be tangible. She finds out what her nominated charity needs and, rather than giving money, gives the gifts that are needed. For example, it may be a toy pack for children who have found themselves in women's shelters with their mothers fleeing from domestic violence or sanitary products for homeless women. When the customers make a purchase, they choose where their charitable donations go.

www.SocialMissionRevolution.com/Cascie-Kambouris

B1G1

An option for donating and building impact in the world that is easy to get involved in is B1G1. It It is an initiative started by Masami Sato here in Australia some 15 years ago. She asked herself, "What would happen if we all gave back just by doing what we do every day?" Originally called Buy1Give1, the idea is that companies choose a specific giving impact attached to a designated business transaction.

Unlike conventional giving models, B1G1 specifically helps small and medium-sized businesses achieve more social impact by embedding giving activities into everyday business operations and creating unique giving stories. Every business transaction or giving can help improve lives for as little as just one cent. Each one of these is referred to as an impact. The business can choose projects that are in alignment with its values. B1G1 has grown into an international movement with thousands of small businesses creating more than 279 million global giving impacts across over 500 carefully chosen charitable causes where 100% of the donations reach the charity and the people in need. All causes are also aligned with the UN Sustainability Goals.

All giving is then trackable so that the business, employees, and customers can follow the impact that they have had. The B1G1 concept is based on 'the power of small', which creates the opportunity for businesses of all sizes to create a positive impact, no matter the extent of their giving resources to make **authentic influence** part of everyday business.

Dr Catherine Yang is a dentist with a passion for making an impact, one smile at a time. When you visit her practice, your smile improves, not only because she physically enhances your smile but also because you contribute to making a difference in the world. With every service Dr Yang provides, an impact is made through her contributions to B1G1. In addition, she encourages her staff to provide a service of excellence by adding incentives to give more significant impact. When they provide good customer service, a financial donation is made to a B1G1 project.
www.SocialMissionRevolution.com/Dr-Catherine-Yang

Johann Nogueira is a successful entrepreneur and founder of Business Authorities. He is committed to making the world a better place and believes it is the role of business to take the lead. In everything his business does, a greater impact is made. The contributions to B1G1 get his team involved in selecting the projects they want to support that align with their business values. When they hold an event, every participant knows that their attendance is making a further impact. At one event alone, they made over one million impacts through B1G1. This involvement keeps the team and employees excited about their work and engages their clients differently.

www.SocialMissionRevolution.com/Johann-Nogueira

Denni Francisco is the founder and designer of Ngali, an Australian Indigenous business working with Indigenous artists, photographers, and creatives to produce clothing, collectibles, accessories, and homewares. Ngali translates to we or us, the collective whole, in several Aboriginal languages. Their commitment to sustainability is to design collections that are ageless, timeless and beyond trend so that pieces can be worn for the longest time, recycled and eventually upcycled. Through B1G1, Ngali provides financial support to the Dot Com Mob to enhance the learning opportunities of children living in remote areas of Australia. This access is vital for young people's education and opens up opportunities to connect with resources and people in the wider world. Through Denni's choices, she works to help Indigenous communities in multiple ways.

www.SocialMissionRevolution.com/Denni-Francisco

Pro Bono work

Giving money is not the only way to be a business with a social mission. Another way is to do pro-bono work - giving your service and time for free. Pro-bono work allows you to take all your skills and expertise and share it with those who may not otherwise be able to afford your service. Doing this also builds relationships with the people you are directly working with and allows you to be an **authentic influence** that will ripple on far more than the time you give.

Anna Osherov is an Eventologist. Her business focuses on teaching business owners and leaders how to build their brand reputation and increase their income by positioning themselves as Niche Industry Influences. While she supports B1G1 initiatives, she felt she could do something more to make a greater impact. She does this by donating her time to run events that create awareness for charitable causes, such as B1G1.
www.SocialMissionRevolution.com/Anna-Osherov

As a family photographer, **Belle Chapman** delights in taking families on an adventure to capture those special fun moments when everyone lets down their guard to play. Her love of photography was influenced by holding on to a few precious photos of her father, who lost his battle with cancer when she was only four years old. The importance of having these memories inspired her to start her social mission, where she does pro bono photography for families who have a loved one diagnosed with cancer. Her passion is to make sure that people who lose family members too early in life have memories that they can physically hold so they remember the moments of fun and love. When you lose someone too early, there have often been difficult times leading up to that. Creating these special memories allows the loved ones left behind to have good times to look back on rather than remember the ordeals. Belle gives her time using her professional skills to ensure families have the type of photos she wished she had with her father.

www.SocialMissionRevolution.com/Belle-Chapman

Erik Bigalk has always felt it is essential to contribute to causes and integrate them into his life. One way that Erik incorporates social mission is to provide pro bono work through his business, Smart Solutions, to charitable causes in assistance with their marketing. This allows him and his team to have direct contact with the positive change they have. As a result, the team are inspired, and their hearts and souls are filled. They measure their success by the difference they have made, knowing that what they've done creates a positive impact.

Through his writing and speaking, Erik inspires others to consider incorporating giving into their business and daily life. As a multi-entrepreneur, business solutionist, speaker, writer and publisher, he creates opportunities for social mission to be an everyday part of his work and life, whether in donations, giving, pro bono work, or charitable giving of time and resources. Passionate about the work of B1G1, he integrates giving through them with all of his projects and business activities to maximise his impact. He has recently started a social enterprise selling coffee to give further support to B1G1 projects. www.BeansforChange.Coffee. www.SocialMissionRevolution.com/Erik-Bigalk

---

Volunteering

Volunteering as a team is a positive way to get everyone in your business involved in a social mission. You can do this in many ways. Getting the team to help out a charity for a day or two gives everyone a sense of purpose and fulfilment. They say, "a change is as good as a holiday."

A day of volunteering breaks the routine and allows your team to think about someone else's needs. It is also a great team-building exercise. They start to see each other in a different light. There is no better way to get to know your team than by volunteering together. You also get to have a direct **authentic influence** on your people as a leader.

Some businesses give their employees one day a month or a quarter as paid work time, where they can give their time to a charity of their choice. This helps boost their morale and gives them the feeling that what they do matters.

Nick Abregu is the CEO of Gorilla Co, a company that specialises in digital marketing. Nick is also the founder of a charity, Winter Care Packages. Every winter since 2015, Nick and his band of volunteers walk the streets of Melbourne and other locations in Victoria with one purpose; to deliver some warmth to those in need. While they hand out items that provide physical warmth, what makes a difference to the recipients' lives is the warmth of human connection. Someone cares. Someone is stopping to have a conversation and to listen. Although Nick has never been homeless, it is something that became his passion.

While there is some separation between the business and charity, Nick's team are all on board to support his endeavours. They volunteer at the fundraising events and go out with him to deliver the packages. His clients and the community are all invited to participate and work with him to make a difference in the lives of those sleeping rough. Working together in this charity helps bring them together and build team spirit. They know that what they do is more than just business.

www.SocialMissionRevolution.com/Nick-Abregu

Social Enterprises

Sometimes a new idea will blossom from unexpected places and in unexpected ways. They can create a whole new direction. A social enterprise is a business set up to drive its social mission. They use business as a tool for the greater good. It is designed around the impact they can have on people and the planet by improving the world. They are an **authentic influence**.

Tiziana De Franceschi is a restauranteur. When her daughter, Crystal, who has Down's Syndrome, asked her if she would train her in hospitality, Tiziana came up with a new idea. When you visit Pizzeria and Trattoria Allegria in the Melbourne suburb of Brighton, you will be greeted and waited on by Tiziana's trainees of differently-abled young people learning life and employment skills that will give them independence.
www.SocialMissionRevolution.com/Tizana-de-Francisco

Nick Savaidis is the founder of Etiko, a social enterprise that pioneered eco-friendly, ethically made fashion and footwear in Australia in 2006. Etiko started as Nick's response to seeing how the fashion industry exploits its workers, including children. Etiko was the first non-food company in Australia to be certified as Fairtrade.

Along with streetwear fashion and footwear, Etiko sells Fairtrade sports balls. Etiko has won awards for being the most sustainable business in Australia in 2008 and won the Australian Human Rights Award in 2016.

What is most important to Nick is creating the social impact he set out to have. On the podcast, Nick talked about his social enterprise needing to be generative - one that generates profit and generates social impact. The more profit you make, the more impact you have.

www.SocialMissionRevolution.com/Nick-Savaidis

Large Enterprises

When you have a large organisation, there are many things you can do. Resources can be directed purposefully into a social mission. It opens up a world where anything is possible. Larger enterprises have a myriad of ways to become an **authentic influence**. It is just about looking at what you are doing and seeing what resources you can deploy in a social mission.

Shelly Galvin is the Corporate Social Responsibility Director at CBT Nuggets, an innovative IT training company. Her role has her intimately involved in creating strategic partnerships with non-profit organisations with a humanitarian agenda. Her company doesn't just write a cheque to those organisations. They get her part-time as a "Super-Temp" to jump into the organisation and support them in any way they need for a set project.

In general, its organisational development, using the skill set that the company has developed along the path of doing business. She helps them set strategies, or fundraising and resource development, consulting, team and leadership development, and assisting with funding the project.

In addition to this, she organises volunteer days for the CBT Nuggets employees, where they go and help an organisation in whatever way they need. Sometimes this means getting dirty, and it isn't at all glamorous. However, these are the most rewarding days for the teams. It connects them to the social mission work that they are doing. Team spirit grows, and productivity increases.

They know that going to work will change someone else's life besides their own. The business grows and goes from strength to strength.
www.SocialMissionRevolution.com/Shelly-Galvin

Creating Opportunities

Many corporations and businesses invest in team-building activities. Some Social Mission Revolution Podcast guests designed businesses that incorporate social mission with team building activities. In a fun experiential way, you can build community spirit and engage in social mission simultaneously. It is a win-win-win opportunity.

Matt Henricks is the CEO and Founder of Henricks Consulting, the Helping Hands Program and the Water Works Program. His passion is helping companies change how employees engage with their work. While he was busy with his own business, he felt the call to do something more - a calling from **beyond the why**.

The Helping Hands Program and the Water Works Program create sessions for businesses or organisations to come together, build up their team spirit, and give to a social mission.

The Helping Hands Program has teams building prosthetic hands for those in need from developing countries. The Water Works Program builds water filtering systems that are delivered to refugee camps where clean water is not available.

These sessions inspire and challenge teams while provide that vital opportunity to make a difference.
www.SocialMissionRevolution.com/Matt-Henricks

Justin Pagotto is passionate about transforming lives, families and social enterprise. His business, Trips Plus, specialises in life-changing group tours. Families or teams travel together to areas in The Philippines where they work together to do aide work that supports the local communities. The tour builds stronger bonds while serving together.
www.SocialMissionRevolution.com/Justin-Pagotto

Choosing Services and Supplies

As a Social Mission Revolutionist, it seems obvious. Yet, this is something we may overlook. Where do we go for our services and supplies that keep you aligned with your values? Suppose you aren't currently in a position to get involved in any other way. In that case, this is a great starting place to becoming a business with social mission.

Supporting other businesses that are actively involved in social mission allows you to piggyback on theirs. Things to consider include

- Are your uniforms made ethically? Are they free of slave labour?
- Are your paper products and stationery eco-friendly?
- What about your cleaning products?
- Can you support supply and service businesses that give a percentage of profits to a charitable cause or have philanthropic activities?
- What Social Enterprises can you support?

Of course, there are many other ways of doing this. Take a fresh look at everything you do. When looking for new suppliers and services, ask if they have a social mission and choose ones that do. My eyes were opened to this with the following story.

Damien Gould is the CEO and Co-Founder of Goodtel, a telecommunications company. After working in the industry for over 25 years, Damien started to think about the possibilities of making a difference through what he knows best. He saw the potential to raise funds for charities by starting his own telecommunications company that did exactly that, raising funds for charities by donating 50% of its profits to charities that help protect the planet and those in need. Goodtel offers customers the opportunity to choose which charity they would like to support from a selection of 11 charities. The charities involved cover the diversity of interests and passions people may have. www.SocialMissionRevolution/Damien-Gould

Dr Stephen Morse has a passion for inspiring leaders and businesses to impact abolishing modern slavery. He believes that modern slavery will not be solved in isolation but rather as governments, businesses, and NGOs work together and engage the real needs of suppliers and workers in the extended supply chain. When I spoke to Stephen on the podcast, it became evident that this is embedded into our society beyond what we may have previously thought possible. His business is Unchained Solutions inspiring you to lead beyond compliance by discovering opportunities to make a lasting impact on those who are impacted by modern slavery. They do this by helping businesses develop a framework for measuring effectiveness, a strategy for remediating instances of modern slavery, and pathways for engaging with social enterprises working on training and employing people at risk of modern slavery. www.SocialMissionRevolution.com/Dr-Stephen-Morse

Sarah Rhodes has a passion for sustainable living. Through her business, Plastic Free SEA, she consults and runs workshops with businesses and corporations. An action plan is created to get your workplace greener and healthier for your team and customers. Customers are focused on sustainability and choose to support businesses and make their purchase decisions accordingly. When your business is the one that ticks all of their boxes, it is the one they choose. www.SocialMissionRevolution.com/Sarah-Rhodes

---

This is just a small cross-section of the many stories of businesses that make a difference through their social missions. More of these stories are available on the *Social Mission Revolution Podcast.* You are urged to hear first-hand the difference having a social mission makes to a business. You will hear many personal stories of individuals who have listened to the call to become an **authentic influence** in the world and have started their social mission. Their stories will inspire you.

A unified vision creates a
long-term commitment
from everyone involved.

CHAPTER 6

Collaborative Prosperity

A business needs to be clear on its purpose, vision and values, as well as how it makes its ultimate impact. When a business has a solid identity, it is time to look at the bigger picture of how it can make changes in the world today. Here is where it can open the doors to a social mission that will leave a legacy.

In my previous book, *Awakened Stealth Leadership*, I concentrated on leadership that inspires teams who change the world. Its focus was on the workplace and inspiring teams to work together in "teamship" to build community.

Building community in the workplace is fundamental to the survival and growth of a business in the 21st century. When people have a sense of belonging, they feel safe and needed. They can grow, develop and initiate new ideas that can lead the business to become an **authentic influence** and have its ultimate impact on the world.

Discovering the social mission that aligns with your business is a journey as a team or community. While you, as a CEO, Founder or Managing Director, can dictate what social mission to be involved in, there is nothing as unifying as working on this together with your staff.

This helps them emotionally attach to the idea and allows you to find the perfect social mission that aligns with the business. This is where you develop authentic **influence** within the business.

When your staff are involved, they want to see this succeed. They feel a greater sense of purpose in their work. They, too, want to make their ultimate impact, and they will do it through your business.

When people come together and let go of their judgments and preconceived ideas, they enable new thoughts and ideas to unfold. They can listen together and allow themselves to be guided as a team by the emerging future. This is where a business aligns its current vision with its highest future potential and creates an enduring legacy.

WHERE IDEAS EMERGE

We all know that when a group of people come together for a common purpose, the results can be more powerful, more successful and go further. What would happen in a business or organisation if the energy and power of going **beyond the why** were multiplied?

> *"We did not put our ideas together. We put our purposes together. And we agreed. Then we decided."*
> – *Sacred Book of Mayans.*

When people come together to create new ideas or make something happen, they often arrive with their agendas. They want to push their ideas forward. But, when you let go of those ideas and are prepared to journey **beyond the why**, with an open mind, open heart and open will, what happens is that new ideas emerge that may not have ever come forward if you did it on your own. Coming together to find that common purpose and flowing from there creates something magical. Here you open up about how you can be an **authentic influence**.

Getting everyone on the same page to work on a new project, develop innovations or solve systemic problems can be problematic in itself. With different and sometimes opposing agendas, or one person coming in with "This is what we are doing" and not even explaining why can be a complete disaster. However, what if we all get out of our headspace and start listening to our hearts and higher selves as one? What if we all are doing it together and connect into our collective wisdom? What if there are no longer multiple whys and multiple agendas, and instead, they are all moulded into one? Then the listening, the deep listening, takes us into a new place altogether, **beyond the why**. New ideas come forth, and innovations start to take shape and old problems are resolved with new systems and pathways. The highest future possibility emerges. Here we connect with the true potential of the business.

You have seen it with new eyes, looked behind every corner. You have listened to what is happening. Together you have come to something new. A new solution or idea in which everyone has participated. When people feel heard and share in developing an idea, everyone owns it. Everyone feels excited and passionate about bringing this idea to fruition.

It is time to allow something new to be born. It is time to act and to create. When a social mission is born from this place, it has the power to make a true difference in the world.

> *When there is a genuine vision (not a vision statement), people excel and learn, not because they are told to, but because they want to. The practice of shared vision involves the skills of unearthing shared pictures of the future that foster genuine commitment and enrolment rather than compliance. In mastering this discipline, leaders learn the counter-productiveness of trying to dictate a vision, no matter how heartfelt. – Peter Senge (2006, "The Fifth*

Discipline: The Art & Practice of The Learning Organization")

A unified vision creates a long-term commitment from everyone involved.

We talk about brainstorming as bouncing ideas off each other. When those ideas stop bouncing off each other and start to merge, we find something powerful that belongs to all. This is the place to find an enduring legacy in the form of a Social Mission.

Working together as a team to find a Social Mission can be both frustrating and extremely rewarding. We all have different passions and ideas. So, how can we get everyone on the same page?

A business takes on a life of its own once it gets going. It is like a child that the founder has birthed. They nourish and guide it along the way. Still, gradually as it matures, it takes on its personality and direction, which can be entirely separate and different from what the founder initially envisioned.

It starts to take on a new look, feel, and direction. If we don't stop and listen to define it, things begin to fall away. Employees will be confused if the founder/owner is still going in the direction they started with and the business is pulling in a different direction.

As it grows, the business gathers its own stories, strengths, values, and a sense of purpose. It is time to gather that all in and discover what that is to focus on the one direction and work with a unified vision to uncover the social mission that is waiting to be born. Very often, this is found **beyond the why**.

Here we are looking for the personality which goes beyond mission and vision statements. They are business. The business's personality guides us to the emotional backdrop of the business. It is not about selling; it is about feeling.

It is what connects with us on a deep emotional level and says, "I want to be involved in this." This is what we need to uncover to find a social mission that truly represents the business and speaks to the heart of all stakeholders.

The unfolding of the social mission for your business is a journey. It is a journey of discovery and renewal. It takes more than one person; it takes the whole team (or a good representation of them).

Once you have a vision and clarity in where you are heading, you want it to be viable. You want it to make the difference you are setting out to make. You want it to be an **authentic influence.** You want it to be an enduring legacy that you can live today and makes a difference for future generations. It is time to look to the future and listen to where it is calling you to go.

How do we listen to the future?

To have all this, we need to follow the seasons. We need to respect the importance of taking time to let go, to release what we thought was necessary and what may no longer be working for us and allow the new and unthought-of to emerge. Taking the time to listen **beyond the why** to where the future wants to lead us is vital if we are to take a business into becoming that flourishing and robust ecosystem that reaches out to the ever-expanding edges and launches into the Social Mission Revolution.

When you can do this together as a community, you will have a unified vision and develop compassionate prosperity. Your team will be on fire, filled with inspirational ideas to take forward and make it happen. They will be fully engaged with the new project and eager to see it come to fruition because it is their project, their ideas, and they know that they will make the ultimate impact together.

In workplaces where the business
focuses on social responsibility,
employees are happier
and more productive.

CHAPTER 7

The Four Seasons of Innovation

Developing new ideas and concepts, whether business or Social Mission focused, can be like the four seasons. Growing into a forest takes time, from planting a seed to allowing that seed time to germinate. It takes commitment to nourish and care for a plant throughout its life cycle.

We can't jump over any seasons in developing your Social Mission. You must allow time for the seed to germinate and discover its path. Winter must come. Too often, the expectation is that it will be Summer and harvest time straight away.

Guess what? It doesn't work like that! When you go through the process step by step, season to season, your new Social Mission gets everything it needs to grow and flourish. It can become an **authentic influence**.

Let's take a journey through the seasons.

This process is based on Theory U, developed by Otto Scharmer. Otto Scharmer is an action researcher, author and lecturer who co-creates innovations in learning and leadership that he delivers through classes and programs at MIT (Massachusetts Institute of Technology) MITx U.Lab, the Presencing Institute. Theory U is a change management system used worldwide by thousands of people from governments, universities, corporations, businesses, communities and individuals who want to make a difference in the world.

Autumn

Autumn is a time of reflection. It is time to look back at what has taken place in the past year and take stock of where you are, what you have learned and how things are coming together. It is time to give thanks for what is and time to start letting go, allowing the new to come forth.

In terms of developing your Social Mission, a time of reflection is required. What are the resources that you have available? What have you done that was successful? What lessons did you learn? And what opportunities are presenting themselves? It is time to research, gather the information and get an idea of the current, complete picture. It is a time for observing and listening to what is happening all around. It is time to look, listen and learn. Gather all your harvest for the on-coming winter, so you are ready and stocked up to go. You are preparing the soil for the planting of new seeds.

EVALUATE

You need to evaluate who you are and what you are doing in your everyday business. Are you ready to take on this new endeavour? How are you situated? Are you running your business in a way that everyone feels that they are valued and can participate in a new adventure? Is your leadership functioning healthily, and are your employees engaged and working together? You need to be sure that you are ready for the disruption this will cause. Consider all these things first.

While having a social mission aligned with your business can significantly increase employee loyalty and commitment, if there is discontent amongst the team, nothing you do will improve your situation. These issues need to be addressed first.

One of the important considerations is to evaluate your purpose in undertaking a Social Mission. Is it because you are obligated to take on corporate social responsibility? Is it so you can improve your business? Or is it because you desire to do something more than making money; you want to make a difference in this world?

You need to be sure that you are in a place where embracing a social mission is possible and will enhance your life and business. You need to make the time for this to happen, and you may need to finance this endeavour.

What will it take for you to do this so that it won't drain energy and resources from the business? The business needs to keep afloat and moving forward. You are taking on a new responsibility that may require extra resources. It is vital to look at this through practical eyes. What is it that you can manage with your current resources?

When you are clear on what resources you have available, it empowers you to step forward. You may find you need more or even less when you get started, but at least you have a "budget." You can readdress this when the project begins. However, if you know that you can commit x hours, y dollars or z resources over the next twelve months, you won't overwhelm yourself and your employees.

How often have you committed yourself to something only to find that you quickly become overwhelmed with the responsibility and workload? You don't want to do this with your business or your new social mission. So, address it now.

Is this going to be a Social Mission where you give a percentage of profit or one where you can provide a portion of time? Or is it something you will go full in and start from scratch?

If you are to succeed in creating a social mission for a business, you need to ensure that you are a healthy organism in the first place. The internal workings need to be in place. The process of developing a Social Mission can help strengthen this, however, take time to review the situation and know where you are placed first.

When leading a business on the journey to uncover its social mission, the place to start is discovering the business's core personality. The uncovering experience reveals more than just the **authentic influence**. You begin to see the critical values embodied in the business – the drivers and unity creators of this community. This is diving **beyond the why** and helps draw people together to align with each other and the company.

You start to discover the themes of values that get people involved. The community may share values of excellence, compassion, collaboration, and ambition, or it could be anything. But these are not manufactured or "wanna-be" values, but ones lived every day.

These values have much more power in influencing how the team within the business operates and develops. They are already ingrained in the everyday. Once they are brought into the light, they can genuinely influence the unity and direction of the future and what that social mission may be.

Connecting with the stories of your employees will unlock hidden gems. Why do they work here? What are their dreams and ambitions beyond their job? What are some of their most fulfilling moments in the workplace? What are they most proud of in their work and about this business?

A new appreciation for the business and each other occurs through sharing stories and experiences of those in the team. The life and story of the business as its own identity starts to emerge.

EXPLORE

Exploring the business beyond what it does on a grand scale and diving into some of those little or unexpected things that happen along the way opens up new opportunities. Here you may find new ways that you can serve your community.

One of the essential aspects to consider is that it isn't always about money. As individuals and as a business, we have specific skill sets available to us. These could be of great value to an organisation or charity already functioning. Even if you are looking at a completely new venture, what are all the different ways your business can get involved and make a difference. For example, the CBT Nuggets story, shared earlier, highlights that one of the opportunities they saw was that they had created systems and structures that improved their business. They could then share these skills by mentoring charities so they become more sustainable.

Another opportunity can be to connect charitable causes with those you know who have the skills that a charity needs. Whatever your skills are, you will have a way to use them as a social mission. Anything is possible when you start to think **beyond the why**.

What powerful opportunities are you already sitting on that you can share with the world?

Looking at your business's stories, strengths, values, and passions as a team to create a **Business Authentic Influence** Statement is an excellent place to start. How does the business have influence, and what can it grow on? When you pull all of this together, you will see how your business can have its ultimate impact on the world. Crafting this as a statement helps give you and your employees a clear focus and inspiration. This is not a statement of empty words, but one that leads the way and gives direction to everything the business is and does.

A **Business Authentic Influence** Statement inspires and uplifts the community. This statement will define the business as its own separate identity. It is beyond a mission or vision statement because it speaks to the emotion; it is the soul of what is and what is possible to achieve.

From here, you have more than a mission, more than a set of values. You have a new definition of purpose, which captures the imagination of employees, customers and the community. It is an inspiration that aspires to positive change and guides you into a new era of innovation, both for business growth and for a social mission.

Working together on exactly how the business has **Authentic Influence** allows new visions to emerge. It may well seem obvious where you are going. A Social Mission that aligns with who you are as a business that speaks your underlying message may emerge. There may be something already in existence that you can get involved in and support. Once you have all this in place, you can confidently move forward and allow new ideas to emerge.

Let's look at this example. If you were about to climb Mount Everest and just started climbing, your chances of survival are pretty slim. If you first ensure that you are healthy, have a good diet, ensure your fitness, and do the training, you are in better standing. If you have the support of your families, friends, and a coach, then you are almost at the summit before you even step foot on the mountain. Then when you add an experienced and trained team to that, you've made it.

If you want to have **authentic influence,** you first need to do the groundwork.

ENCOUNTER

Looking at who you are, why you do what you do, and how you can have your ultimate impact starts to allow new ideas to present themselves as to where you are heading with a Social Mission. It would be effortless just to come in and say this is what we are going to do and jump straight into it. However, if you think about the seasons, that would be like planting seeds in Autumn expecting to jump to Summer to receive the bounty of fruit.

It doesn't happen that way. You need to allow the seasons to unfold naturally and work with them. This is when you get the best results.

Without the proper preparation and time to find just the right mission that aligns with your values, vision and how you can be an **authentic influence**, you may do a botch job of it all. It may not completely capture the heart and soul of your business.

This is about going **beyond the why** and capturing the true soul of your business.

When your Social Mission aligns with the mission and vision of your business, it guides your direction. It is easy for employees and consumers to connect the dots. You feel a passion that enlivens you. The two integrate into one.

When you see them as entirely separate, without any interlocking pieces, it will feel like you are running two businesses that divide your time. When the two are in alignment, it will flow.

Take a closer look at where your business excels. Go beyond the obvious. This is where the magic is. What are the emotions that are evoked by your business? What are the more profound problems you solve?

The right Social Mission will align with who you are and the business's values. It needs to align with the statement you developed earlier to know that you have all the skills and strengths required. Once you have that, you need to understand the background stories of the situation. Then you will have an idea and are sure that it is right for you. You need to explore. You need to understand the who, the what, and the how's of a situation before you embark on the journey.

Then you are ready to start exploring the possibilities.

Taking time to understand the issue and problems that your new Social Mission solves is vital. You need to get to the core of the problem and see the actual cause, not just what it appears to be.

Unless you explore the truth of a situation, you may not be helping at all. You can't walk into a community and say, "This is what you need." Efforts like this are often a waste of time and resources and don't solve the real problems as they haven't reached the cause. Instead of being an **authentic influence**, you could become a negative influence. You need to take time to learn all of the good, the bad and the ugly parts of a situation, as it is, without judgement. It is essential to know the people you are helping so you can see the truth of a problem from the community's eyes and not your own.

Knowing what has created today's problems will help you let go and look for new solutions for tomorrow. This will help you gain insights and understand why things aren't working. Letting go clears the path for something new to come in.

An old saying, "Give a man a fish, and he'll eat for a day. Teach him to fish, and you feed him for a lifetime." That is the essence of how powerful this can be. We can look at something and think we have the solution, but we can't answer if we don't know the cause of the problem.

Take time to consult with those involved in this situation. How does it look from all perspectives of all the stakeholders? Get a clear overview of what is going on.

This is where many people go wrong. What will happen if you keep going without looking at the root problems and clearing out the debris? You need to see the situation for what it is.

Having a clear picture of the problem or situation will help guide you to relevant solutions. When ideas come to you, you will know whether they are inspired ideas or just your brain working overtime to think up solutions. True clarity will come. This is so important if the influence you have is to be an **authentic influence.**

Autumn is about looking, listening and learning. Gather all your harvest for the on-coming winter, so you are ready and stocked up to go. You have prepared the soil for new seeds to be planted.

Winter

Winter is a time of rest and allows nature to prepare for the new life.

As we move into winter, it becomes a time to let go. Letting go of what hasn't worked, letting go of the things that may be holding the development back. Letting go of our agendas. If you hang on to old ideas and models, you might just miss out on reaching that highest potential. To be an **authentic influence,** you have to be willing to listen to something new, something **beyond the why** that can take you to where the future is calling you to go.

This is vital if you are to take full advantage of the new ideas and inspiration that will be revealed. You may find you are inspired to go on a completely different tangent.

Let go of what was and allow the new to be planted within. Take time to reflect and renew yourself, when this is done as a team, even more, powerful visions of what can come forth. As the group starts to dialogue their ideas, new ones grow on top of each other, they expand, and the vision grows into limitless possibilities.

There comes the point where no one can pinpoint where an idea has come from as it is in the process of working together that the idea has spring boarded. Here we can recognise the importance of having set rules of engagement.

Everyone needs to feel safe in expressing themselves. They need to feel safe in the discomfort of dialogue that may get heated as ideas evolve and develop. However, the result is that everyone feels that they have had a part in creating this, and they are all passionate about making this come to pass. They have an emotional investment in ensuring that the best of this comes through. Now it is time to put it into action.

ENVISION

Now that you have gathered all of your information, it is time to retreat. You need to let go of your agendas and allow yourself to connect with the collective wisdom. When you allow yourself to listen to the emerging future new ideas that will serve the cause will come forward.

While you now have a clear picture of what has been happening and all the ins and outs, you can't just jump ahead and try to fix the problem. It is time to retreat. You need to download and let go of everything in your mind to prepare yourself to rest.

Anyone who has had any illness understands the importance of allowing yourself to come to rest. You do it every day. You let go at the end of the day and sleep – well, some of us do!

You need to be refreshed and rejuvenated before starting a new day. It is the same with this process. You need to stop and reflect on where you have been and allow the busyness of your mind to come to a rest.

When our mind is rested and clear, new ideas emerge. The limitations of your mind don't hold you back. Anything is possible when you journey **beyond the why**.

This is like cutting loose from all the chains that have held you back, letting go of that load of past ideas and perceptions. Yet, it is more than that. As you prepare yourself for new things, it allows you, as a team, to gather up all that you have and find those gems that are in there that can move you forward. It is clearing space to make way for the new.

It's like a clogged artery; if you don't clear out the path, it gets more and more clogged, and you have a heart attack. So, you have a choice, keep piling up the way things are and clogging up more and more, or you address the problem at the cause, make changes in your life and allow the blood to flow freely, giving you a new lease on life.

Otto Scharmer and Joseph Jaworski from MIT – authors of *Presence,* researched the world's greatest living minds. This included 150 interviews with leaders, entrepreneurs, and innovators who are actively involved in change processes in companies, governments, and communities.

They were asked about their process for coming up with new ideas. They all had the same basic process that served them time and time again. It is in letting go and listening to where the future is guiding them.

When do you get your most significant moments of inspiration?

If you think about it, it's often when you're in the shower, going for a walk or a run, or in the middle of the night. It is usually when you have let go of what is happening around you and have cleared your mind. One of the most inspirational spaces is when you are out in nature, just reconnecting with the oneness of all and with ourselves.

Spending time in retreat with your team and allowing time for thoughts to flow is part of the process.

Unfortunately, the result of not letting go of what is in our mind, releasing those thoughts that go around and around, is that you keep getting the same results that nobody wants. You're not allowing those new ideas to come to you. Even if they do, you are so caught up with old concepts and methodologies that making new ideas and innovations work beyond their minds is a waste of time.

Can you see how important it is to first go through the process of pulling everything together during the Autumn phase? This allows you to make the most of winter. You know who you are and what you have to offer. Brilliance can now unfold.

Too often, you are trying to solve tomorrow's problem with yesterday's solutions. This rarely works. To be an **authentic influence,** you need to be ready to listen to where the future is leading you. You need tomorrow's solutions today.

ENFOLD

When you have the spark of an idea to work with, it is time for opening up dialogue and unravelling the future that is revealing itself. A unified vision is waiting to be created – the ideas will start to spark from one person to the next and flow through the whole group creating a concept that belongs to everyone. Ideas and innovations that evoke passion within your team will develop a culture of performance and profit. Without innovation, you have no growth.

It is time to journey **beyond the why** and listen to where the future is guiding. An awareness of new opportunities that are before you start to come forth. New ideas, new ways of operating, new understandings. It is connecting with the collective wisdom available to us all if you just take the time to let this unfold. Here you are connecting to your natural source of presence, creativity and power. You are sensing what wants to come forth and allowing it to come into being.

During the lengthy Melbourne COVID-19 lockdown in 2020, **David Rooney** would take his one hour allowed exercise time walking with his friend Jordan Meachen. During this time, they would talk about their dreams and hopes.

Where would they go now? What would they do to pull themselves out of this long spell that had decimated their lives? As they talked about depression and their experiences, thoughts and ideas percolated. They wanted to fight the battle against depression somehow. An idea was sparked as they spoke and listened to each other.

They are now starting a skincare brand that deals with acne, as they see this as impacting people prone to depression. Committed to making a difference in this area, the profits are dedicated to assisting in conversations around mental health. Their brand is "Boring Without You."
www.SocialMissionRevolution.com/David-Rooney

The process of allowing new ideas to come as a team can be potent. They can transcend all preconceived limitations. You are tapping into the wisdom and inspiration of all; this is what those great minds, mentioned earlier, were doing. They listened to the guidance that came from beyond their mind and jumped into the flow. This is what you need to tap into if you are to impact the world. Here is where you connect with the emerging future.

Don't expect to be anything other than ordinary in your mission if you don't do this. You might have some good ideas, but you're like everyone else without tapping into this flow. You will not be able to be that **authentic influence** that is in your destiny to make.

Maybe you don't like the weather in Autumn and Winter. You would like to jump straight from Spring to Summer. However, DON'T. You will have regular old brainstorming that will not take you to your highest future potential without them. You will waste time and resources. You also miss out on tapping into authenticity and connectedness that can only emerge when you open your heart, mind and will together and journey **beyond the why** to be guided into the future.

Spring

As Spring takes hold, new life begins to blossom. Seeds are pollinated, fruit starts to develop, and new growth is everywhere.

If you have rugged up and experienced Autumn and Winter, you have journeyed **beyond the why** and are ready with new ideas. It is crucial to act as quickly as possible and do some trials on whatever has been decided.

Of course, some planning is required, but if you spend too much time planning and none in testing, you put all your eggs in one basket with nothing to show for it. Make it a priority to get your idea started, trialled, and tested.

Then the process of evaluating the idea can take place quickly. You can see what may, or may not, work. In this process, you can improve and make changes needed as you progress.

You aren't 100% invested in having ideas work at this stage. There is more room for error and mistakes to occur without it being costly. Therefore, if it doesn't work, other ideas can be tested. Inevitably, some things won't work. You need to be prepared for this and allow for failure to happen. In failure, we learn and develop new and greater ideas.

EXPERIMENT

Once you have the idea on the table, you need to unpack it and understand how it will work. It is time to crystalise the vision and intention. Will this create the desired **authentic influence**?

It is time to create a prototype by linking the head, heart, and hand. A prototype is an opportunity to experiment on a small scale. This is where you can make changes and alterations, where needed, to the original idea. Try it out and see how it works, feels and what response it gets before committing fully.

Introducing "Brew sessions" to help develop new ideas, inspiration and innovations that are coming forth –

listening, reflecting and conceptualising. Brew sessions bring the team together and have them working on an equal footing. Here they can discuss where they are at and how to move forward to inspire and motivate everyone.

There is something magical and mystical about the experience of sharing tea. This is the perfect analogy of collaboration and "brewing" new ideas and developing concepts, opening up to the magic and mystery that allows ideas to flow – just like tea.

Brew sessions are more than sitting around having a cuppa and a chat. They are about supporting each other on projects and direction. These sessions are about exploring an idea, a situation, or a challenge with others in the team. You open up the experience of getting to the core of what is happening. Brew Sessions are a way to support each other's ongoing journey and work with your current challenges. They allow the team to work together in an open and meaningful way to look at a situation from many different viewpoints.

In these sessions, you dive in deep to uncover the situation's actual background, then allow the observations and new thought processes to be revealed. When new ideas come to us, it is something you need to act on NOW! So how are you going to do and get it into action?

Let's get the idea happening. Fail fast and succeed quickly to work on your vision and allow it to develop further. It gives you something to put in front of people and generates feedback that will help you to evolve and shape your idea. Get moving with ideas quickly and develop them as you go. They don't have to be perfect to start. Strike while the iron is hot!

When the idea of Chocolate and Coffee Day came to me, I realised that it was up to me to make it happen. I had no idea what to do. I just jumped in, doing what I could. I promoted the concept on social media and spoke to people about it. That was what I could do at that moment. I took the small steps.

When you listen to the Social Mission Revolution podcast, you will hear this again and again in many of the stories. It is repeatedly a case of let's get this started, and we learn along the way.

When you get a glimpse of something, you can quickly lose it if action isn't taken. Taking the time to explore and unpack this new concept helps bring it to life. When you take quick action on your ideas, it creates momentum, keeping the passion and the vision alive. Getting going quickly and trialling things in small ways will soon give you the answers and responses you need on what is and what isn't going to work.

It is no longer theoretical; it is happening. You get your answers quickly and relatively cheaply. You get to find out if this is how you will have **authentic influence.** When the team can see things happening, it helps them stay connected with the inspiration.

When a new vision or idea appears, you need to take time to get to know it; you need to look at it from all sides, feel into it, and breathe it in. Like an artist preparing to paint a scene, you don't just take one look and paint it.

Have you seen the television program *Landscape Artist of the Year* on the Sky Arts Channel? A group of artists are taken to a location, and they all have four hours to paint or create this scene on a canvas. The variation in results is remarkable. A variety of different mediums are used. While most use paint, either oils or watercolours, others use mediums such as ink, stencilling and even collage.

Even though every piece of work is different, we recognise the scene as this location. Each artist sees it in another way. They will pick up on different hues in colour and light. They will choose different angles and other views to depict the feeling of the day. They focus on additional details and use different strokes to tell the story that they see.

When we look at any situation, we can be blinded by the forms of what we are used to seeing. It is not until we step out of the problem that we can start to look around and see the truth of what has been happening. Sometimes it takes someone from outside to offer another perspective that will open our eyes. We may get to view the same circumstance from different viewpoints and angles, just like the other painters present.

By working together and getting different viewpoints, we start to piece together a complete picture of what is in front of us. What one person sees as the view and what the next person sees can be completely different. When we work together on this masterpiece, we can get a complete picture that works for all.

This is where you see the true vision unfold. While you are in the flow, it is easy for us to continue to unpack the ideas and concepts and allow them to form. It gives us clarity on the mission, enabling us to share with others and get them on board. It is time to trial out ideas and start on a small scale.

Now that you have a clear vision of something that invokes a great passion within you and your team, you can move into the next step of getting others involved and being an **authentic influence** on them.

Summer

Agriculturally, the crops are fully grown. They are reaching the pinnacle of maturity and coming closer to harvest time. This is where we see the fruits of our labour – where **authentic influence** blooms.

EMERGE

This is integrating the Social Mission from the inside out. You have seen, through prototyping, what has worked and are now ready to share on a larger scale. Now is the time to integrate your social mission through the whole organisation and include it in your branding and marketing.

The value of this cannot be understated. When everyone in your business is on board with the Social Mission, it lifts their sense of fulfilment and gets them in on the action. They will find ways to be involved in making it successful.

Now you have a purpose and a passion that belongs to the whole of the business, not just one or two people. The aim is 1) to get support to make the mission successful and 2) motivate your team.

In workplaces where the business focuses on social responsibility, employees are happier and more productive. They have greater client retention, generate innovation, and have a more significant influence and reputation in society. All this then relates to greater profitability. So, it gives the business a competitive advantage.

And let's face it – it feels good.

Research and consulting firm IO Sustainability found, in their study project *ROI, Defining the Competitive and*

Financial Advantages of Corporate Responsibility and Sustainability, that companies who integrate social impact into their business were able to:

- enhance sales by as much as 20%
- increase productivity by 13%
- reduce employee turnover by half
- protect against litigation risk at a value equivalent to the cost of insurance worth up to 4% of the company's value
- increase the company's share price by up to 6%
- create a "reputation dividend" worth up to 11% of market capitalisation
- reduce financial risk, the cost of equity, and the cost of borrowing.

The overall effect and value to the business are directly proportional to how much the social mission is integrated.

Once your social mission penetrates your business and your employees are involved and excited, it is ready to launch into the community. Now incorporate your social mission into your branding. You can do press releases, if you choose, to share your Social Mission with the world.

Keep it in front of your mind in everything you are involved with and do. Make sure that leaders are visibly participating in this venture and all the team get the opportunity to join in.

Affiliate with organisations and supporters of this mission, find other organisations and individuals who support this cause and affiliate yourself with them. Create new collaborations and connections. You never know what you can do together and how significant that impact will be.

Do this right. Present it from a sincere and authentic place; then, you will have **authentic influence**. If you are doing this only to entice your customers to spend more money with you, they will see right through you. Your social mission needs to be a calling greater than money.

EVALUATE

Then you are back at the evaluation stage again.

Evaluation is an essential step. You must evaluate what you have done and how you are going every step of the way. Once you have your compassionate project up and running, you need to ensure that it is self-sufficient and continues running. Is this complete? Do you continue? Is there something else you now need to address?

Evaluating keeps everyone on their toes. You want this to be an ongoing legacy that you will be proud of forever. Continual renewal and involvement will support the project and keep it fresh to motivate your team and your customers.

Defining your Social Mission is not a set and forget concept. It needs to be reviewed regularly to ensure it aligns with your intent. With a cycle of evaluation and the lessons learned, you can diagnose, improve and maybe even venture into new territories. When you are clear on what is and isn't working, you have a powerful tool to move forward, grow and inspire. You have created a legacy. You are an **authentic influence**.

You come back to the consulting from the Explore stage. It is essential to revisit looking and listening to what is happening and questioning if it fulfils the solution, you set out to create. This changes along the way. You may need to change tactics entirely at some stage, so keeping a regular eye on what is happening is vital.

An example of this is the "Thank You" company. They set out to create a sustainable business to direct all profits to providing water to people in developing countries who could not access clean water. They saw the potential in bottled water, as Australians were buying vast quantities of it. They set up their business, and it started to bloom. However, when they stopped and reflected on what they had created, they realised they had got something very wrong. They were contributing to the problem of waste with single-use plastic water bottles. They stopped selling water immediately and refocused their business on their growing range of personal products. "Thank you" is still a growing business that donates profits to worthwhile causes in developing nations. Consumers can follow where the money from their purchase goes from a code on the packaging.

Where do you go from here? Keep on track and develop new projects and directions. Be prepared to journey **beyond the why**. Just because you have done one thing doesn't mean you have to stop. The next place you are called to serve may indeed be **beyond the why** and take you into being an even more significant **authentic influence**.

The most amazing and seemingly impossible ideas may eventuate but remember:

> *"Only those who can see the invisible can do the impossible"*
> *– Jeffrey Fry.*

CHAPTER 8

Free to Fly

When I was ten years old, my family found a cockatoo chick blown out of its nest in a windstorm. He was too young to fly, and his parents had no way of getting him back into the nest. He came home with us.

My father named him Fella. I became Fella's surrogate mother, feeding him with a specially prepared baby cockatoo mush. Times were different then, and rehabilitating and releasing a bird into the wild was thought impossible. Fella became our pet.

Fella never learnt to fly. In fact, he fears flying. On occasion, he would suddenly find his wings and take off. Fear would take over him, and he would land on the nearest thing – a tree branch or the neighbour's roof. He would sit there and wait for me to climb up and try to coax this frightened bird down.

Most of the time, he can just come out of his aviary and wander around in the backyard without concern that he will take off. He spends some time chewing on whatever he can find, pulling out weeds (and things that aren't weeds,) then wanders back to his aviary and safety.

Fella doesn't have to fend for himself, but what has that cost him? He could easily take off at any time, go exploring, and have the life that a cockatoo should have; however, his life is safe as it is.

You could say that my father was well-meaning when he brought Fella home all those years ago. He and Fella had a close relationship. He loved this bird, and he gave him everything he needed. They had a strong bond. Now that my father has passed and Fella lives with me, we have renewed our bond.

Did you know that sulphur-crested cockatoos can live up to 100 years in captivity? When my first grandchild was born, my daughter surrounded him with cockatoo paraphernalia. I think she is preparing him to be the next custodian of Fella.

I think about Fella's story as I reflect on Social Mission. It is one thing for us to be well-meaning, to go out and help someone, wanting to make a difference in their lives. However, we don't want to lock them up in a cage of reliance in doing so. It is far from ideal to lock them in a cage where they become solely dependent on you. Fella has a choice. He could have flown away; however, he has stayed. He doesn't know how to fend for himself. He doesn't know or understand what it is to be a wild cockatoo, like the cockatoos that come to visit him. He doesn't even have the skills to communicate with them. Why don't they respond to him when he calls them Charlie?

The aim of a social mission should always be to set the bird free. Give them what they need to nourish them, build their strength, teach them how to go out in the world and survive, and then open up the door and set them free.

In their freedom, they are always free to return for advice and encouragement. However, they are not ours to keep in a cage for our amusement or in our need to give.

When you set one bird free, you are free to give to someone else, have an **authentic influence** on more people, and have an even greater impact on the world.

A Social Mission Revolutionist
is waiting to be born in each of us.

CHAPTER 9

Conclusion

The Social Mission Revolution is all about contribution. It is about finding the purpose within the community that allows everyone to contribute and feel like what they do matters. You matter, so I matter – my contribution matters. You can do something that makes you feel worthwhile. We can do something that creates the world we want to live in.

A business with a social mission inspires change, consumers, and its employees and their families. It creates a following of people who believe in their cause. People become devoted followers of the brand because it speaks to their hearts by serving humanity. When Compassionate Prosperity is embraced, a business becomes an **authentic influence**.

There is no denying that developing a social mission for your business can be a big task. There will be times when it disrupts everything. However, it may be the most rewarding and satisfying thing you will ever do in your business. It will bring people together and give them focus and purpose in their work. It will help your business stand out as one that is worth supporting. Most of all, you will have built a legacy worth living and leaving.

We have explored what it means to have a social mission in this book and looked at various examples from the podcast *Social Mission Revolution*. There are many more stories to explore. Each one of them is uniquely beautiful. They have been designed to align with the unique attributes and personality of the business and those involved. Like these, your social mission will reflect who you are and the business you have already built.

As you listen to each podcast, you will be inspired and motivated to think further about what you and your business are being called to do in the world. Be open to journeying **beyond your why**. You may find something that sparks your imagination, or maybe you would like to support someone else's cause. Whatever your choice, it is a good choice.

Invite those around you to also listen to the podcasts and be inspired. Whether they are in business or not, there is something for everyone. A Social Mission Revolutionist is waiting to be born in each of us. When it is born in you, get in touch, and maybe you will be the next guest on the Social Mission Revolution.

I hope that this book has inspired you and given you fuel for your journey for developing Compassionate Prosperity and becoming an **authentic influence.**

Bibliography

Cone Communications 2010, Cone Cause Evolution Study, https://www.conecomm.com/2010-cone-communications-cause-evolution-study-pdf

Gallup 2021, *State of the Global Workplace Engagement Report 2021, Gallup Headquarters, Washington, USA*

Glavas, A., and Kelley, K. 2014, 'The effects of perceived corporate social responsibility on employee attitudes, Business Ethics Quarterly, cambridge.org.

Henderson, M. 2015, Culturing Success: How workplace culture drives innovation in Australia's leading SMEs. Microsoft, Australia.

McCrindle Research Pty Ltd, 2014 *Australian shoppers, prefer ethical and Fairtrade products: study*, http://www.smartcompany.com.au/growth/42189-australian-shoppers-prefer- ethical-and-fairtrade-products-study.html.

Post, Dr S. 2011, *It's good to be good: 2011 5th annual scientific report on health, happiness and helping others,* The International Journal of Person Centered Medicine.

Post, Dr S. & Niemark, J. 2007, *Why Good Things Happen to Good People*, Broadway Books, New York City.

Putting, A. & Saini, S. 2018, *Awakened Stealth Leadership*, Mohindra Publishing House, India.
Rochlin, S., Jordan, S., Bliss R., Kiser. C. YEAR, *Project ROI: Defining the Competitive and Financial Advantages of Corporate Responsibility and Sustainability*, IO Sustainability, Projectroi.com.

Senge, P, Scharmer, O. & Jaworski, J. Flowers, B.S. 2008, *Presence*. Currency, USA

Senge, P. 2006 *The Fifth Discipline: The Art & Practice of The Learning Organization*, 2nd edn, Currency, USA.

Index

About the Author

Andrea Putting is an international speaker, author and trusted advisor to Authentic Influencers. Through her keynote speeches, books, programs and podcasts, she guides businesses in building co-creative communities and adopting a social mission. While the cause is serving humanity and the environment, the effect is growing leaders and visionary teams that strengthen business, develop a community within the workplace, and inspire consumers who want to support businesses that care.

After studying Naturopathy and Homoeopathy, Andrea started her own business as an early adopter of the online world. When she sold this business, she entered the workforce as an employee. Here she discovered a world that also needed healing. Her deep exploration led her to the Social Mission Revolution.

Since 2019, Andrea has been championing the causes of passionate people making a difference in the world through her podcast, *Social Mission Revolution.* The podcast highlights inspirational people and businesses who have an **authentic influence** on the world through social mission.

When we combine our passions, something magical can be created. Andrea's passions and values came together to create her social mission where people can come together to break down barriers. Chocolate and Coffee Day for Religious Harmony began on 15 December 2015. Chocolate and Coffee Breaks evolved in 2020 to transform situations where there are any feelings of nonacceptance and misunderstanding into building a community spirit.

Andrea was awarded the Toastmaster of the Year in her local club in 2016. She was honoured with awards as the Best Volunteer and Best Tribe Member in global awards with Speakers Tribe in 2020 and nominated as Best Leader in 2021. She received a Wordsmith award at the Innov8 Awards, 2021.

Andrea's writings have been inspiring and challenging people over the internet for over 20 years. As an author, she and has written, *Awakened Stealth Leadership*, inspired by more than four decades of experience in leadership, provided chapters in various books and written many published articles.

Andrea Putting lives in Melbourne, Australia, amongst the gumtrees, kangaroos and cockatoos with her husband and pet cockatoo, Fella. She has two adult children and two grandchildren who keep her jumping in puddles.

For further information on
Compassionate Prosperity
visit www.AndreaPutting.com

Chocolate and Coffee Breaks

C hocolate, coffee and conversation – what a delicious combination! It incites deep sensuous emotions and experiences, which take us out of the daily grind and lift us into a place of belonging and acceptance. It is a simple way to make a difference and become an authentic influence.

If you can make one person smile and lift their spirits when they feel lonely, isolated, or depressed, something shifts in the whole universe.

Reaching one person is simple. Chocolate and Coffee Day for Religious Harmony and Chocolate and Coffee Breaks create connections that allow this to happen.

Sharing chocolate and a cuppa with someone is part of our daily life. It transcends all cultures. There is something about sitting with someone else with a cup in our hands. In doing this, we meet each other as equals.

The warmth of the liquid allows us to open up and speak more freely and compassionately than we might otherwise do. It brings us into a place of listening, ready to hear the other's story. It allows us to be prepared to open up to find the similarities that help us connect.

When we share these simple pleasures of life, something magical happens. We can break down barriers that divide us.

Sharing in **Chocolate and Coffee Breaks** opens us up to creating communities where we all feel a sense of belonging, are accepted and are provided with an opportunity to contribute. These are essential parts of our being. Wherever there are any nonacceptance and misunderstanding feelings, it is time for a **Chocolate and Coffee Break**.

Chocolate and Coffee Day for Religious Harmony is held each year on 15 December. However, any day of the year is a good day for a **Chocolate and Coffee Break**.

Visit www.ChocolateandCoffeeBreaks.com for ideas and conversation starters and explore how you, your community or your business can get involved. You can also invite Andrea Putting to facilitate a Chocolate and Coffee Event for you.

Social Mission Revolution Podcast

Social Mission Revolution Podcast began in 2019. During this time, Andrea has interviewed people from all walks of life who are involved in social mission. Their stories are varied and cover a wide diversity of worthy causes.

The podcast can be listened to at
www.SocialMissionRevolution.com
or watch on YouTube.

Apple Podcasts   Spotify   Podchaser   Pocket Casts

Google Podcasts   Overcast   Deezer   Listen Notes

Amazon Music   Stitcher   Player FM   Podcast Index

iHeartRadio   Podcast Addict   Podfriend   RSS Feed

Castro   Castbox

www.ingramcontent.com/pod-product-compliance
Lightning Source LLC
Chambersburg PA
CBHW032044040426
42334CB00038B/611